SCIENCE ANSWERS

Forces and Motion

FROM PUSH TO SHOVE

Heinemann
LIBRARY

H www.heinemann.co.uk/library

Visit our website to find out more information about **Heinemann Library** books.

To order:

☎ Phone 44 (0) 1865 888066

▤ Send a fax to 44 (0) 1865 314091

▤ Visit the Heinemann Bookshop at www.heinemann.co.uk/library to browse our catalogue and order online.

First published in Great Britain by Heinemann Library, Halley Court, Jordan Hill, Oxford OX2 8EJ, part of Harcourt Education.

Heinemann is a registered trademark of Harcourt Education Ltd.

Editorial: Sarah Eason and Georga Godwin
Design: Jo Hinton-Malivoire and
  Tinstar Design Ltd (www.tinstar.co.uk)
Illustrations: Jeff Edwards
Picture Research: Rosie Garai
  and Liz Eddison
Production: Viv Hichens

Originated by Ambassador Litho Ltd
Printed and bound in China by WKT

ISBN 0 431 17496 2 (hardback)
07 06 05
10 9 8 7 6 5 4 3 2

ISBN 0 431 17504 7 (paperback)
08 07 06 05 04
10 9 8 7 6 5 4 3 2 1

British Library Cataloguing in Publication Data
Cooper, Christopher
Forces And Motion – From Push To Shove.
– (Science Answers)
531.1'1
A full catalogue record for this book is available from the British Library.

Acknowledgements
The Publishers would like to thank the following for permission to reproduce photographs: Corbis **p. 29**; Corbis/Orban Thierry **p. 11**; Corbis/Joel W. Rogers **p. 21**; Corbis/Nigel Rolstone **p. 26**; Corbis/Robert Y. Kaufman **p. 20**; Corbis/Tom Stewart **p. 13**; Corbis/Bettman **p. 28**; Corbis/Douglas Peebles **p. 7**; Corbis/George D. Lepp **p. 9**; Corbis/Hughes Martin **p. 4**; Getty Images/Arthur Tilley **p. 5**; Science Photo Library **pp. 17, 18**; Science Photo Library/Takeshi Takahara **pp. 14**; Getty Images/Jack Ambrose **p. 23**; Trevor Clifford **pp. 8, 12, 25**; Tudor Photography **p. 22**.

Cover photograph of snowboarding reproduced with permission of Corbis/David Stoecklern.

The Publishers would like to thank Robert Snedden and Barbara Katz for their assistance with the preparation of this book.

Every effort has been made to contact copyright holders of any material reproduced in this book. Any omissions will be rectified in subsequent printings if notice is given to the Publishers.

Contents

Any words appearing in bold, **like this**, are explained in the Glossary.

About the experiments and demonstrations

In each chapter of this book you will find a section called 'Science Answers'. This describes an experiment or demonstration that you can try yourself. There are some simple safety rules to follow when doing an experiment:

• Ask an adult to help with any cutting using a sharp knife.

• Mains electricity is dangerous. Never, ever try to experiment with it.

• Do not use any of your experimental materials near a mains electrical socket.

Materials you will use

Most of the experiments and demonstrations in this book can be done with objects that you can find in your own home. A few will need items that you can buy from a hardware shop. You will also need paper and pencil to record your results.

What are forces?

What are forces?

We live in a world of movement. The sky, the air and the sea are never still. Even the ground beneath your feet is **constantly** moving. Everything around you is made up of tiny particles called **atoms**. Even the smallest grain of sand is made up of millions of atoms, and they are constantly in motion. The chair you sit on may seem perfectly still, but it consists of atoms that **vibrate** all the time.

Other objects move in ways that we can see. Your bicycle rolls downhill unless you press the brake. When you press the brake it slows down. When you hit a ball with a tennis racquet, the ball starts moving or, if it is already moving, changes direction. Cars and aeroplanes use powerful engines to push them forwards and up into the sky.

Sliding downhill

The force of **gravity** affects everything on Earth. It is making this skier slide downhill. The snow is slippery, so when the skier starts moving the snow exerts only a weak force, called **friction**. The force of gravity is stronger than the forces slowing the skis, so the skier goes faster and faster. As the skier travels faster, the force exerted by the snow increases. When it equals the force of gravity, the skier keeps travelling at a **constant** high speed.

Exerting a force

Whenever an object speeds up, slows down or starts moving in a different direction, it is because a **force** has acted on it.

We say that a force is being 'exerted'. You **exert a force** whenever you pick something up, or throw it, or push it or pull it.

Kicking a ball

You often exert forces yourself. This boy is exerting a force on the ball by kicking it. The ball will change direction when it is kicked. The harder the ball is kicked, the more quickly it will travel in the new direction.

What happens when you push or pull an object?

You can see the effects of **forces** whenever you push something. If you push a shopping trolley it will tend to move away from you. If you pull the shopping trolley, it will tend to move towards you.

The muscles of your body are **exerting a force** and the object being pushed or pulled is responding to that force.

Opposing forces

Exerting a force does not always make something move. This is because there is nearly always more than one force acting on any object. For example, if you tried to push or pull a heavy block of concrete lying on the ground it would probably not move at all. There is also a lot of **friction** between the block and the ground. Friction is the force created whenever two objects rub against one another. In order to move the block, your push or pull would have to be greater than the friction force between the block and the ground.

The amount of friction between two materials depends on how strongly they are pressed together. The heavy block of concrete presses strongly on the ground and creates a strong friction force. A smaller, lighter block would press less strongly and create a weaker friction force. The amount of friction also depends on what two types of material are being pressed together. The heavy block of concrete resting on ice would slide easily because ice is very smooth.

The scientist Isaac Newton came up with some rules that describe forces and their effects. His first rule is called **Newton's First Law of Motion**. It says that an object will stay still or continue moving in the same direction at the same **speed** unless a force is applied to it. When you push a shopping trolley you are applying force to it, causing it to move. It would keep moving in the same direction at the same speed except that friction between the wheels and the ground slow it down.

Forces in nature

These boats are being pushed along by the wind. The wind is exerting a force on the sails of the boats, and the force is pushing the boats through the water. The boats would stop moving if they accidentally ran on to the beach – the force of friction on land would be stronger than the force of the wind. The water causes less friction because it can flow and so can get out of the way of the boats.

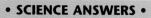

EXPERIMENT: How can we reduce the effects of friction and move objects around more easily?

HYPOTHESIS:

If the amount of rubbing between the objects is reduced, they should move more easily.

EQUIPMENT:

A medium-sized book (or similar-sized object), a length of string about 60 cm long, a wide elastic band about 10 cm long, a packet of plastic drinking-straws (straight – not the 'bendy' kind).

EXPERIMENT STEPS:

1 Pass the string through the elastic band, and then tie the ends of the string in a loop.
2 Place the book on the tabletop and loop the string around the book, so that you can pull the book along.
3 Hold the elastic band, and pull the book across the table, trying to keep it moving steadily. Notice how much the elastic band stretches. The more force that is needed to pull the book, the more the elastic band will stretch.
4 Now make a 'road' of straws. In the same way as previously, drag the book along this 'road', with the straws acting as rollers. Does the elastic band stretch more or less than before?
5 Write down what you saw.

(See next page for conclusion.)

CONCLUSION:
You should have found that the elastic band stretched less when the book moved on the rollers. There is less friction because the book and the straws do not rub against each other – the rolling straws move with the book. Large rollers are sometimes used to move heavy objects.

A heavy load

It needs a big force from the locomotive to get these heavy freight cars moving. But once the train is moving, it needs a very strong force to make it stop. So trains like this have to have good brakes, to apply that force.

How can forces change the shape of objects?

Forces affect different materials in very different ways. It depends on how the materials **resist**, or **react** to, the applied force. If you push your finger into a piece of modelling clay, the clay hardly resists at all, and is pushed aside. When you pull your finger away, the clay does not go back to its original shape – it stays put in its new shape. The **atoms** in the clay are held together by chemical links that prevent them from being easily separated, but do not hold them **rigidly** in place.

The atoms in a hard material such as wood are held together by links that keep them rigidly in place. There is almost no change of shape when you apply a force to a piece of wood, if the force is not very strong. If you apply a very strong force, the wood shatters.

What makes things bouncy?

Rubber and many plastics are **elastic**, or 'bouncy'. When you stretch or squeeze them, their shape changes. At the same time they pull or push back. Thus, when you stretch an elastic band, it becomes harder and harder to stretch it the longer it gets. When you release the force, an elastic material bounces, or springs, back into its original shape.

Elastic materials behave as if their atoms were linked by springs. When the material is stretched or squeezed, the 'springs' try to get back to their original length and bring the atoms back to their original position. It is rather like a trampoline, in which the bouncy canvas surface is supported by springs, which always try to pull it back into its proper flat shape.

Springing back into shape

The material in a tennis ball is elastic. When it is hit hard, the ball is squashed but it springs back into shape as it leaves the racquet.

EXPERIMENT: What makes some balls bouncier than others?

HYPOTHESIS:
Balls will be more or less bouncy, depending on whether they are made of plastic or latex, on whether they are solid or have air in the middle, and on how heavy they are.

EQUIPMENT:
Ruler or tape measure, a wall that you can temporarily mark with pencil or chalk, and bouncy balls of several different materials. You might find a tennis ball, a ping-pong ball, and various balls from a toy shop, including a novelty 'super-bouncy' ball.
You will need another person to help you.

(Continued overleaf.)

EXPERIMENT STEPS:

1 Make a mark about shoulder-height on the wall.
2 Arrange the balls into groups so that all the balls in one group are about the same size.
3 Drop each ball in turn from this mark. Make sure you drop it rather than throwing it, otherwise you will be applying extra force to the ball.
4 The other person marks the height that the ball rises to after its first bounce. The more elastic the ball is, the higher it will bounce.
5 For each group of balls, make a note of the types of ball and the heights they reached. Was the ball hollow? Did it have a solid core? Was it made from hard plastic or softer rubber?
6 Write down what you saw.

CONCLUSION:

No ball is perfectly elastic: none of them rises to the same height that it was dropped from. But some rise higher than others.

Now clean the pencil marks off the wall!

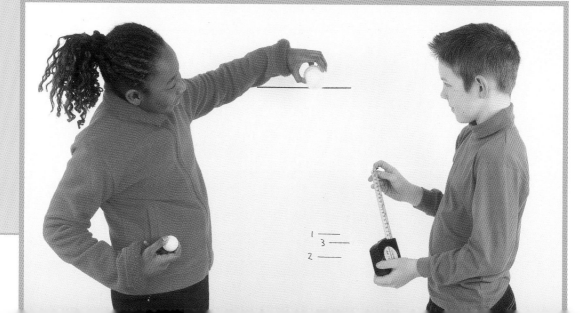

How can we make objects move faster and slower?

If there were no **forces** acting on it, an object would keep on going at the same **speed** – for ever! This is because, according to Isaac **Newton's First Law of Motion**, an object continues at rest or moving at **constant** speed in a straight line unless acted on by an outside force.

However, when a force is applied to an object, as long as it is not cancelled out by an equal and opposite force, it will make the object go faster or slower. Or, it will alter its direction. This is **Newton's Second Law of Motion**.

What do 'action' and 'reaction' mean?

Isaac **Newton's Third Law of Motion** states that:

To every action there is an equal and opposite reaction.

'**Action**' here just means a force. '**Reaction**' means an opposing force that is generated by it.

When you press down on a tabletop, the force you press down with is the action. The table presses back upwards – otherwise your hand would keep going down. That upward force by the table is the reaction.

Why does everything need a force to keep it moving?

Without a force to keep it moving, an object can be slowed or stopped by other forces, including **friction** and **gravity**. A car or truck rolls to a halt if the engine is turned off, because of friction with the road. A bicycle comes to a stop when you stop pedalling because of friction with the road surface. A rocket starts to slow down when its engines stop firing, because of the gravitational pull of the Earth.

What a drag!

When a car is moving, it experiences a strong force holding it back, caused by the air rushing past it. This slowing force is called 'drag'. Engineers study the drag on a new car design by putting the car, or a model of the car, in a wind tunnel. They measure the force that acts on the car when a strong stream of air blows over it.

EXPERIMENT: Is Newton's Third Law of Motion right?

HYPOTHESIS:
For every action there is an equal and opposite reaction.

EQUIPMENT:
A large plastic drink bottle, four drinking straws (two different sizes and thicknesses), modelling clay, thin card.

EXPERIMENT STEPS:
1 Place a ball of modelling clay large enough to cover the mouth of the bottle around one end of one of the smaller straws.
2 Place the end of the straw and the clay inside the mouth of the bottle to seal the bottle.
3 Cut two strips of thin card. One piece should be 14 cm long and 2 cm wide, and the other piece needs to be 7 cm long and 2 cm wide.
4 Sellotape the two pieces of card to form circles.
5 Put the largest card circle on the base of the larger straw so that it looks like it forms a hoop around the straw.
6 Put the smaller circle at the end of the large straw, forming a hoop.
7 Put a small ball of clay into the end of the large straw like a cork.
8 Insert the small straw that is attached to the bottle inside the large straw. Squeeze the bottle and see what happens.
9 Write down what you saw.

CONCLUSION:
When you squeeze the plastic bottle, the air inside is blown through the small straw and into the larger straw. Since the air cannot escape through the plugged end of the large straw, pressure builds up and makes the straw shoot forward. This proves **Newton's Third Law of Motion**: for every action there is an equal and opposite reaction.

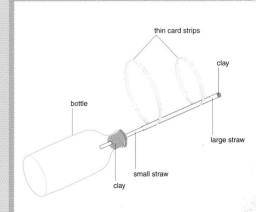

thin card strips

clay

bottle

large straw

small straw

clay

Why do things fall to the ground when you drop them?

Everything near the Earth tends to fall to the ground unless something prevents it. This tendency is called **gravity**.
An object falls to the ground because of a downward **force** called its **weight**. Weight is called a gravitational force. It is greater for a heavy object and less for a lighter object. A brick has more weight than a cotton ball.

Gravity stops us from falling off the Earth and floating into space, and makes water run downhill.

Is everything affected by gravity?
All objects, in space and on the Earth, are attracted to each other by gravity. The Moon, planets, Sun and stars all have gravity that pulls things towards them.

You can see and feel the effects of the Earth's gravity. You see things fall, pulled down by gravity. When you carry something, you can feel its weight, which is the result of gravity. You can feel the pull on the Earth on you too, when you sit on a chair and feel the pressure of the furniture against your body.

How strong is gravity?
The strength of the gravitational force is different between different objects. One thing it depends on is the **masses** of the objects (the amount of **matter** contained in them). An 18-wheeler truck contains much more mass than you do, and so the pull of the Earth on it is much greater than its pull on you. This is just another way of saying that the truck is very much heavier than you.

The strength of the gravitational force also depends on the distance between the objects. When they are farther away from each other, the force is weaker. If you were an astronaut floating in space, as far away from the Earth as the Moon is, the Earth's gravitational tug on you would be less than a thousandth of what it now is.

Escaping gravity

An object that is trying to travel into space needs to have very powerful engines. But even the engines on this Space Shuttle do not enable it to escape the force of the Earth's gravity completely. Instead, it stays in a circular path, or orbit, circling the Earth.

Earth, Sun and Moon

Gravity is the reason why the Earth goes round the Sun. It is also the reason why the Moon goes round the Earth. The Moon has much less mass than the Earth, so its gravitational force is less.

Astronauts who land on the Moon feel lighter. The amount of matter in their bodies (their mass) is the same as on Earth, but the effect of gravity on that mass – that is, their weight – is smaller.

Why do some things float?

In a tub of water, each drop of water is held in place by the **pressure** (pushing **force**) of all the drops of water around it. There are sideways, downward and upward pushes, combining to give an upward force. This force balances the **weight** of that drop of water exactly – keeping it in place.

What is displacement?

When you place a piece of wood gently in a container of water that is filled to the top, some of the water overflows. We say that this water is **displaced** by the piece of wood.

When the displaced water has gone from the container, the water that remains in the container pushes the object in exactly the same way that it previously pushed on the water that has been displaced. So there is an upward force on the object equal to the weight of the displaced water.

The wood is less **dense** than water – that is, its weight is less than the weight of an equal volume of water. So the weight of the wood is less than the upthrust that it now 'feels'. The wood moves upwards.

Archimedes' principle

This can be summed up in Archimedes' principle, named after the Greek scientist who first discovered it more than 2000 years ago. He studied liquids, but it applies to all fluids, or materials that flow (liquids or gases):

The upward force on an object in a fluid is equal to the weight of the displaced fluid.

How do submarines work?

Submarines have large tanks that are filled partly with water and partly with air. When the submarine needs to dive, air is pumped out of the tanks, which take in more water. Air is very much less dense than water, so replacing some of the air with water makes the submarine as a whole more dense. In other words, the submarine becomes heavier and sinks beneath the surface.

To get back to the surface quickly, compressed air stored onboard is blown into the tanks, pushing water out and making the submarine less heavy, so that it rises.

Can an object made of heavy iron float?

Iron is **denser** than water – that is, any piece of iron weighs more than the same **volume** of water. If you put a solid piece of iron into the water, the upward push is not enough to keep it at the surface.

But if the iron is a hollow shape, like a bowl, the **density** of the iron bowl now includes the air inside it. Air, of course, is less dense than water. Ships float, even though they are built from dense iron and steel, because there is so much air inside them.

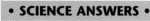

EXPERIMENT: How can I make an object float and sink in water?

HYPOTHESIS:
An object may float if it displaces more water, and sink if it displaces less.

EQUIPMENT:
A large (1-litre) plastic drink bottle, a bowl, a large pen-cap, several paper-clips.

EXPERIMENT STEPS:
1 Fill a bowl with water. Attach the paper-clips around the opening of the pen-cap until it will just about float upright in the bowl – trapping an air bubble.
2 Fill the bottle nearly to the top with water and float the paper-clipped pen-cap in it. Screw on the bottle-top.
3 Now squeeze the bottle: the 'submarine' pen-cap will sink to the bottom. Release the bottle and it floats to the surface.
4 Write down what you saw.

CONCLUSION:
Squeezing the bottle means you are exerting pressure on the water inside – that is, pushing on the water. The water in turn exerts pressure on the air bubble, making it smaller in the pen-cap. This means that the air bubble displaces less water, and there is less of an upward force on the bubble. So the pen-cap 'submarine' sinks.

What is pressure?

The air around us is like an ocean of gas. This 'ocean' is called the Earth's atmosphere. The air has **weight**, and presses on you and everything around you. It pushes you from all directions. This push is called **pressure**.

Air is much less **dense** than the same **volume** of water. But the atmosphere is hundreds of kilometres deep. The column of air above a single square **metre** of the Earth's surface has a **mass** of over 10 tonnes (over 10,000 **kilograms**).

What is the pressure at the bottom of the ocean?

As you go deeper in the ocean, there is more water on top of you. More water weighs more. This means the water pressure increases. This diver's suit contains air at high pressure to push back against the water pressure of the ocean. But not even the most advanced diver's suit would enable anyone to go to the bottom of the deepest parts of the Pacific Ocean. The sea floor there is 10 km (6 miles) deep and the pressure is 1000 times atmospheric pressure at sea level.

DEMONSTRATION: Crushing proof.

Air pressure increases when the air is heated. You can prove this to yourself by following the steps below.

EQUIPMENT:
An empty plastic drinks bottle, water from a hot tap.
Warning: Do not use boiling or very hot water from a tap or kettle, which is dangerous and will melt the plastic bottle.

DEMONSTRATION STEPS:
1 Half-fill the bottle with hot water.
2 Screw on the cap and shake up the bottle to warm up the air inside and mix it with water vapour (water in gas form).
3 Then pour out the liquid and quickly screw the cap back on.
4 Now run water from the cold tap over the bottle. As the air inside cools, and the water vapour turns back into liquid water, the bottle is squashed and crumples.
5 Write down what you saw.

EXPLANATION:
Hot air and water vapour were at a higher pressure than cold air and water. As the contents of the bottle were cooled, the pressure inside the bottle fell. The pressure of the air and water vapour inside no longer balanced the pressure of the air outside. Therefore, the bottle was squashed.

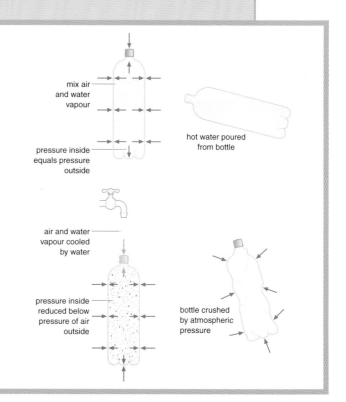

How can forces work for us?

The phrase 'simple machine' has a special meaning to scientists. It is just a device that changes the direction of a **force**, or its strength, or the place where you apply the force.

A simple machine can be an everyday **device** such as a **lever**. An example of a lever is a crowbar. You push downwards on one end of a crowbar and the other end rises, lifting, say, a paving-stone. Your push is called the **effort**. The **weight** of the paving-stone is called the **load**.

There are other sorts of simple machine that do not use levers. For example, **pulleys** are used in industry. These are arrangements of wheels and cables that increase the pulling power of engines and human muscles.

How can a person lift a car?

One type of car jack uses a handle that the person turns. Every time the handle turns, the car is raised a little way. After many turns the effort (the force applied by the person) has moved a long way while the load (the heavy car) has risen only a short way.

How do simple machines work?

Simple machines are usually (though not always) used to increase the strength of the force that the user exerts. In these cases the machines are designed so that the effort moves farther than the load. This is the secret of the simple machine: a small effort moving a long way can result in a large load moving a small distance.

A big haul

This winch on a boat is being used to wind in a rope holding a sail that is being strongly pulled by the wind. **Friction** holds the rope on the drum of the winch. The person using the winch uses a handle as a lever to turn the drum.

• SCIENCE ANSWERS •

EXPERIMENT: How can one person overcome the strength of several people?

HYPOTHESIS:
A simple machine can be rigged up to increase the force exerted by the lone person.

EQUIPMENT:
Two broomsticks, garden rakes or similar poles, length of rope at least 6 m long, assistance of several people.

EXPERIMENT STEPS:
1 Lay the poles parallel on the ground, about 30 cm apart.
2 Knot the rope to the end of one of them.
3 Loop the rope back and forth at least six times over the two poles as shown. The rope now makes a 'cage' around the poles.
4 Take the free end of the rope while the other people pick up the poles.
5 Pull on the rope as hard as you can while your opponents try as hard as they can to pull the poles apart.
6 Write down what you saw.

CONCLUSION:
If the rope is looped around the poles enough times, a child can defeat several adults. The secret is that the effort (the force you apply) moves much farther than the load (the force your opponents apply).

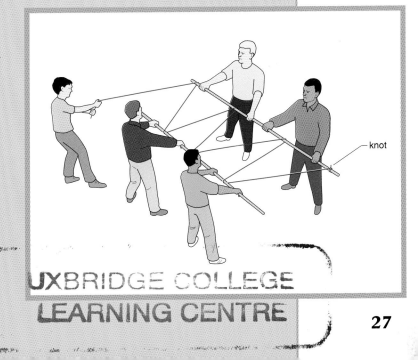

knot

People who found the answers

Archimedes of Syracuse (287–212 BC)

Archimedes of Syracuse was possibly the greatest scientist of the ancient world. He made many mathematical discoveries and studied **forces** and movement. In what we now call the 'Archimedes principle' he stated that a body in a liquid experiences an upward force equal to the **weight** of the liquid **displaced**.

Archimedes is said to have invented fearsome weapons of war to defend his home city of Syracuse against Roman armies, such as cranes that lifted whole ships out of the water, and huge mirrors that concentrated sunlight on to ships, setting fire to their sails.

Isaac Newton (1642–1727)

Isaac Newton gave us our modern understanding of force. He was studying at the University of Cambridge in 1665 when there was an outbreak of plague and he had to go home temporarily. The story goes that while home, he saw an apple fall from a tree. He had the idea that the same force that pulled it to the ground was keeping the Moon moving around the Earth. This went against the long-held idea that the heavens obey completely different laws from those that hold on Earth.

Newton went further in his 'law of universal **gravitation**'. This states that every piece of **matter** in the universe attracts every other. He also discovered his three laws of motion (see page 13). With these and other revolutionary discoveries, Newton was able to explain the movements of falling objects and of the Moon and planets, as well as the rise and fall of the tides.

Amazing facts

- All forces are produced by four fundamental, or basic, forces. **Gravity** is one fundamental force. Electromagnetism is another (sometimes electromagnetism appears as electric forces, at other times as magnetic forces). Two fundamental forces, called the strong and the weak nuclear forces, operate in the centre of the atom. The strongest fundamental force is the strong nuclear force and the weakest is gravity. The ratio of the strength of the strong nuclear force to that of gravity is 1 followed by 39 zeros – that's one thousand trillion trillion trillion (one trillion is one million million).

- **Atoms** can be 'photographed' with a microscope that measures forces instead of focusing light. The atomic force microscope (AFM) contains a strip of springy material about a tenth of a millimetre long. The strip is moved across the surface of a sample being studied, about a millionth of a millimetre away. The surface attracts the strip more strongly where the gap between them is smaller. The tiny force at each point is measured. A computer turns this information into a picture of the surface.

- The greatest amount of controlled **force** produced by human beings is developed by the Space Shuttle. At launch, two solid-fuel booster rockets generate about 1400 **tonnes** of thrust each. (A force of 1 tonne is equal to the **weight** of an object that has a mass of 1 tonne.) As well as that, there are three main engines burning, each generating about 170 tonnes. That adds up to over 3000 tonnes of force.

Glossary

action force – for every action there is an equal force in the opposite direction called the reaction

atom one of the tiny particles of which matter is made. It consists of still smaller particles.

constant always the same

dense having a high density

density how much mass an object or material has per unit volume

device something made for a special purpose

displaced push aside. An object placed in liquid displaces some of the liquid.

effort force exerted by a person, an animal or a machine to make something move

elastic describes something like latex, which goes back to the same shape after having been pulled or squeezed out of shape

exert a force make or produce a force and push or pull something with it

force influence that alters or moves an object

friction force of attraction between atoms that tends to stop two objects or materials moving when they are in contact with each other

gravity force of attraction between every particle in the universe and every other particle. Also called 'gravitation'.

kilogram scientific unit of mass. Symbol kg.

lever device consisting of a bar that can be turned around a fixed point. You can use it for altering the point at which you exert a force, or the direction of the force, and, often, its strength.

load force exerted by an object on a person, or an animal or a machine that is trying to make that object move

machine anything made to help human beings do some task, such as a car, a computer, or an electric drill, or to give information, such as a clock

mass amount of matter in an object. It is measured in kilograms.

matter anything that has mass and occupies space

metre scientific unit of length and distance. It is defined as 1/299,792,458 of the distance that light travels in a vacuum in one second. Symbol m.

Newton's First Law of Motion this states that an object stays at rest or keeps moving in a straight line at a constant speed, unless acted on by a force

Newton's Second Law of Motion this states that an object tends to accelerate in the direction of a force exerted on it; the greater the force, the more it accelerates, but the more mass the object has, the less it accelerates

Newton's Third Law of Motion this states that for every action (force) there is an equal and opposite reaction (opposed force)

pressure amount of force per unit area

pulley simple machine made of linked wheels that increases the force that a person can exert

reaction force that is produced by an action and that is equal and opposite to it

resist when an object or a material resists something moving, it tends to slow it down – for example, water resists the fall of a diver

rigid not changing shape

simple machine any device, such as a lever or a pulley, that alters the strength or direction of a force, or the place at which it is exerted

speed how fast something moves. It is measured in metres per second.

tonne unit of mass equal to 1000 kilograms. Symbol t.

vibration fast backwards-and-forwards motion

volume amount of space; it is measured in cubic metres

weight measure of force exerted on an object by gravity

Index

More books to read

Science Topics: Forces and Motion, Anne Fullick and
    Chris Oxlade (Heinemann Library, 2000)
Science Projects: Forces and Motion, Simon de Pinna
    (Hodder Wayland, 1997)